Against th...

Four True Life Stories About
COURAGE

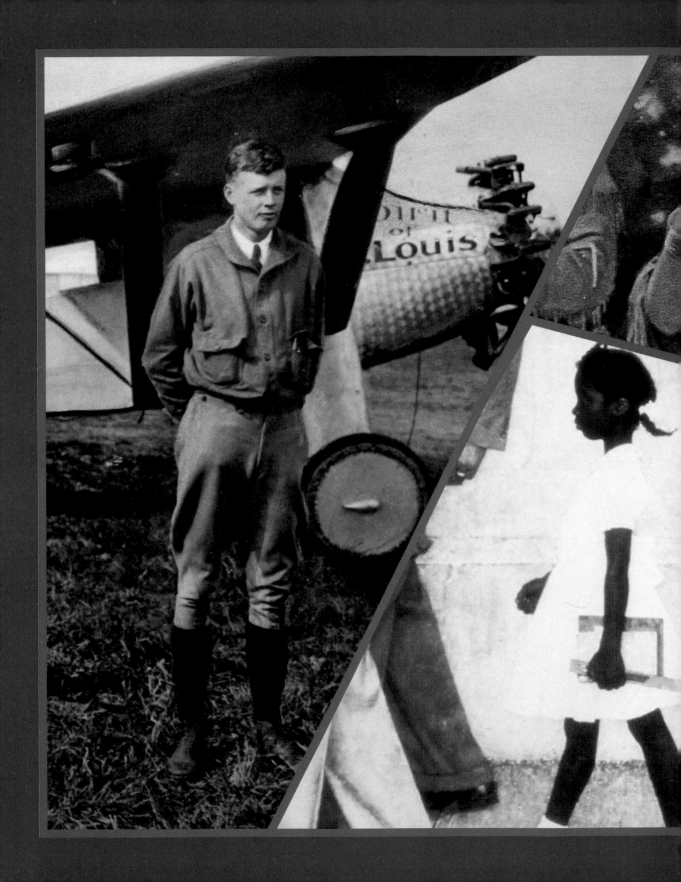

COVER ILLUSTRATION:

Justin Ray Thompson

PHOTO CREDITS:

AP/Wide World—Andy King, p. 9; Damian Dovarganes, p. 10; Orlin
   Wagner, pp. 14-15; David J. Phillip, p. 16; Corcoran Gallery, p. 27;
   Steven Senne, p. 28; other: p. 24
Christopher Reeve Paralysis Foundation—Dana Fineman, p. 6
Granger Collection—pp. 12, 18, 21, 22
Hulton|Archive—p. 8

Copyright © 2002
Kidsbooks, Inc.
230 Fifth Avenue
New York, NY 10001

Manufactured in the United States of America

Visit us at *www.kidsbooks.com*

VALUES IN ACTION™

Against the Odds

Four True Life Stories About
COURAGE

Courage is the inner strength to carry on through great difficulty, pain, or fear. In this book, you will meet four extraordinary people who persevered against great odds. Their courage has inspired millions of other people to overcome hardships and challenges in their own lives.

Christopher Reeve
by Denise Rinaldo

Sacagawea
by Susan E. Edgar

Charles Lindbergh
by Denise Rinaldo

Ruby Bridges
by Denise Rinaldo

Christopher Reeve

born 1952

Christopher Reeve was flying high. World famous for playing the Man of Steel in four Superman movies, he was strong, healthy, and happily married with three loving children. Then tragedy struck. Reeve—a talented horseback rider—took a disastrous fall from his horse. When he woke up five days later, he was paralyzed and unable to breathe on his own. Many people would have given up, but Reeve vowed to walk again someday. From his wheelchair, he now raises money for research into spinal-cord injuries. Reeve's courage in the face of adversity and his desire to help others have made the former movie Superman a real-life hero.

A Super Start

Christopher Reeve was born September 25, 1952, in New York City. He grew up in Princeton, New Jersey, with his mother, stepfather, brother, and two half-brothers. Christopher was the oldest of the four boys.

Christopher caught the acting bug at age 9, when he was cast in a local production of a Gilbert and Sullivan play. He also loved sports. By all accounts a tough competitor, he skied, raced sailboats, played goalie on his high school hockey team, and took fencing lessons. After high school, Christopher studied theater at Cornell University and the Juilliard School. By the time he graduated, he had several professional acting jobs under his belt. He dreamed of life as a star, making blockbuster movies and acting in serious dramas.

> *"When the first* Superman *movie came out, I was frequently asked, 'What is a hero?'* . . . *My answer [then] was that a hero is someone who commits a courageous action without considering the consequences.* . . . *Now my definition is completely different. I think a hero is an ordinary individual who finds the strength to persevere and endure in spite of overwhelming obstacles."*
>
> —Christopher Reeve

His big chance came when he landed the lead role in a high-profile movie, *Superman*. The 1978 hit made him a full-fledged star. In the next 17 years, he made 31 films for theaters and TV, including three *Superman* sequels. He also appeared in stage plays. At first, it was rough—audiences identified him only with Superman, and some critics made mocking remarks about the Man of Steel when he played more serious roles. In time, however, things began to turn around. By 1991, critics were praising his work and he had met the love of his life, actress/singer Dana Morosini. In 1992, the two married and had a son, Will. (Christopher also has two older children, Matthew and Alexandra.)

Then, in May 1995, Christopher went to Culpepper, Virginia, to ride in a horse-jumping competition. He easily cleared the first two jumps, but something spooked his horse at the third. The animal stopped suddenly and Christopher was thrown over its head. He landed on his forehead and his neck snapped back.

The Power to Overcome

Doctors later explained Christopher's injury to him: Basically, his skull had been disconnected from his spinal column. An operation could reconnect them, but not restore his ability to move. In his autobiography, *Still Me*, Christopher recalls saying to Dana: "Maybe we should let me go." Dana looked him in the eye and said, "You're still you. And I love you." Christopher has said that Dana's words made living possible.

After his surgery, Christopher began intensive physical therapy, which continues to this day. He has to practice tasks that most people don't even think about—like breathing on his own and sitting up. At first, he says, he was terrified almost all the time. He was completely dependent on a mechanical ventilator, which pumps air to his lungs through a hole in his

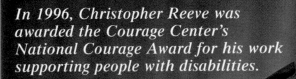

In 1996, Christopher Reeve was awarded the Courage Center's National Courage Award for his work supporting people with disabilities.

throat. If the tube popped off, he could die.

Eight months after his accident, Christopher was able to go home. Since then, he has dedicated himself to raising money for research on spinal-cord injuries. "Thank God I can be helpful rather than just take up space," he has said. "It gives me a sense of purpose." In the year 2000 alone, the Christopher Reeve Paralysis Foundation gave almost $4 million to researchers. He also has made a difference by testifying before Congress: The federal budget for

Christopher Reeve with his wife, Dana, and their son Will

Spinal-cord Injuries

The spinal cord, which runs down your back, is a ropelike mass of nerve cells that conduct information to and from the brain. Signals to the brain enable it to identify conditions in the world around you. For example, they let you feel cold when you step into icy water. Signals from the brain tell your body when and how to move—to hop out of that water, for instance.

When a spinal cord is damaged, the brain may send signals saying "move," but the arms and legs don't get the message.

Unlike many parts of the body (such as the skin), spinal cords do not grow new cells to replace damaged ones. Scientists are searching for ways to change that—to help injured spinal cords heal.

spinal-cord research has more than doubled since he began speaking out. Now an expert on spinal-cord injuries, he is convinced that doctors will find a cure. He works with physical therapists, so he will be ready to walk if a breakthrough is made. He has made progress—he now can move one of his shoulders and can breathe for three hours without a ventilator.

Christopher has begun to act again. He starred in a TV movie, *Rear Window*, and provided the voice for King Arthur in an animated film, *The Quest for Camelot*. In 1996, he directed his first film, *In the Gloaming*, for cable television. It was nominated for five Emmy Awards.

Christopher Reeve's biggest contribution, however, is his courage in moving forward with hope. It has inspired people all over the world.

Life Lines

1952 Christopher Reeve is born in New York City, September 25.

1978 Christopher stars in the movie *Superman*. A hit with critics and audiences alike, it makes him a star. In the following years, he performs in many films and sometimes on stage.

1995 On May 27, Christopher falls from his horse, Eastern Express, and is paralyzed.

1996 Christopher appears, in his wheelchair, on the Academy Awards show, introducing a segment about films that tackled social issues. He says, "There is no challenge, artistic or otherwise, that we can't meet." The audience gives him a two-minute standing ovation.

1996 Christopher's best-selling autobiography, *Still Me*, is published.

1999 The Christopher Reeve Paralysis Foundation is founded.

Explorers Lewis and
Clark with Sacagawea,
their invaluable guide

Sacagawea

born about 1787 • died 1812 or 1844

S acagawea *(SAK-uh-gah-WEE-uh)*, a young Native American woman, faced many great challenges. Traveling with Lewis and Clark's team of explorers in 1805-1806, she helped blaze trails and gather information about vast areas of uncharted wilderness west of the Mississippi River. Today, more monuments have been dedicated to Sacagawea and her courageous spirit than to any other woman in U.S. history.

Far From the Shining Mountains

Sacagawea was born into the Shoshone *(shoh-SHOH-nee)* Native American culture in the late 1780s, around the time George Washington became the first president of the United States. The Shoshone lived in the Bitterroot Valley, near the present-day border of Montana and Idaho. They called it the Land of the Shining Mountains, because the surrounding peaks glistened with snow most of the year. The Shoshone were nomads, moving from place to place as they hunted for food.

When Sacagawea was about 12 years old, a band of Hidatsa Indians raided her village, killing several men, women, and boys. Several girls, including Sacagawea, were taken far away from the Shining Mountains to a place called the Three Forks, an area in North Dakota where three rivers flowed together. The girls were made to work as slaves at the Hidatsa village.

The Hidatsa had a very different lifestyle from the Shoshone. The

> *"Through the [translations] of LaBiche, Charbonneau, and Sah-cah-gar-we-ah, we communicated to them [the Shoshone] fully the [objectives] which had brought us into this distant part of the country."*
>
> —Meriwether Lewis, in his journal entry of August 17, 1805

Hidatsa were farmers, who settled in one place and tended the land. Young Sacagawea soon learned to plant and harvest crops, like Hidatsa women. When she was a teenager, the Hidatsa sold her to Toussaint Charbonneau, a French Canadian fur trapper who lived near Three Forks. Charbonneau made her his wife.

Corps of Discovery

In the winter of 1804, an expedition team known as the Corps of Discovery arrived at Fort Mandan, near Three Forks. It was led by Meriwether Lewis and William Clark, who had been sent by President Thomas Jefferson to explore the western region of the North American continent. Both Lewis and Clark kept journals, recording everything they experienced along the way. Lewis was a naturalist—he studied plants and animals, and wrote about the people they met. Clark, a mapmaker, charted the routes they took. The Corps spent the winter at Fort Mandan.

Lewis and Clark needed an interpreter—someone who could speak Native American languages. They were willing to pay $500 and 320 acres of land. Charbonneau could speak French and Hidatsa, and his wife spoke Hidatsa and Shoshoni. François

This Corps of Discovery monument, which stands in Kansas City, Missouri, features Sacagawea along with Lewis, Clark, and York, Clark's slave.

LaBiche, already a member of the Corps, spoke French and English. So, it was settled; Sacagawea, Charbonneau, and their two-month-old son joined the Corps. The group left Three Forks once the snow melted in the spring of 1805. The Corps of Discovery, 30 members in all, welcomed the newcomers. Having a woman and a baby in the group was a sign to anyone they met along the way that the Corps was on a peaceful mission.

Sacagawea soon proved more courageous and helpful than anyone had expected. For instance, when a boat capsized, her quick-witted action rescued precious papers and supplies. Her knowledge of the terrain was helpful, too: With her baby strapped to her back in a cradleboard, she led the explorers safely through rough territory unknown to them. Using old Indian trails, she shortened their trek by hundreds of miles. When the Corps arrived in the Bitterroot Valley, Sacagawea asked local people where the Corps could buy horses to haul food on the long journey. Among the group, Sacagawea was surprised and thrilled to find her brother, whom she had not seen for years. After a brief reunion, the group moved on. Sacagawea may have wanted to stay in her homeland, but she

15

knew that the expedition was important and that her assistance was invaluable.

The Corps of Discovery traveled as far west as Oregon's Pacific coast, then back to North Dakota—more than 4,000 miles in 16 months. The expedition was a great success. Both Lewis and Clark wrote about Sacagawea's courage and praised her interpretive

Dollar coins, first issued in 2000, honor Sacagawea's place in American history.

Saving the Day

Sacagawea had not been with Lewis and Clark long before the young woman proved herself a worthy member of the team. On May 14, 1805, a sudden storm blew up while some of the team were in boats on a river.

Lewis and Clark watched from shore as their men, yelling and fighting panic, struggled to keep a boat carrying irreplaceable maps, papers, and supplies from going under. Through it all, Sacagawea remained calm.

"The Indian woman," Lewis later wrote, "to whom I ascribe equal fortitude and resolution with any person on board at the time of the accident, caught and preserved most of the light articles which were washed overboard."

and trailblazing skills. In a letter to Charbonneau, dated August 20, 1806, Clark wrote: "Your woman, who accompanied you [on] that long, dangerous, and fatiguing route to the Pacific Ocean and back, deserved a greater reward for her attention and services on that route than we had in our power to give her."

According to some reports, Sacagawea died of fever in 1812, just six years after her heroic journey. Other reports, however, have her living to a great old age, dying in 1884. Regardless of when she died, her story of courage lives on. In 2001, the U.S. Mint issued a dollar coin bearing Sacagawea's image. She also was given the honorary military rank of sergeant for her service to her country.

Life Lines

1787? Sacagawea is born in the Bitterroot Valley, an area in what is now western Montana and eastern Idaho.

1800? Sacagawea is kidnapped by Hidatsa Indians.

1804 The Corps of Discovery, led by Meriwether Lewis and William Clark, leaves St. Louis, Missouri, to explore the West.

1805 Sacagawea gives birth in February. Soon afterward, she, her husband, and child join the Corps of Discovery. After a long, hard trek, the group reaches the Pacific Ocean on November 18. In 1806, Sacagawea returns to her village on the Missouri River.

1812 According to some reports, Sacagawea dies on December 20. (Other reports say that she lived until April 9, 1884.)

2000 The U.S. Mint issues a new, gold-colored dollar coin featuring an image of Sacagawea.

Charles Lindbergh

born 1901 • died 1974

When Charles Lindbergh was a boy, he would gaze up at the clouds and daydream. "How wonderful it would be, I thought, if I had an airplane," he later wrote. In his wildest dreams, however, he did not imagine that he would become the most famous aviator of all time—the first to make a nonstop solo flight across the Atlantic Ocean. Nor could he know that his fame would take a terrible personal toll.

"Daredevil Lindbergh"

Charles Augustus Lindbergh was born on February 4, 1902, in Detroit, Michigan. He grew up on his family's farm near Little Falls, Minnesota. From the time he was a young child, Charles loved danger and proving his own bravery. His father encouraged this. When Charles fell into the Mississippi River as a boy, his father didn't jump in to rescue him. He simply called to young Charles to teach himself to swim. He did.

After a year at college, Charles pursued his dream of flying. He wound up in Nebraska at Ray Page's Flying School. On April 9, 1922, he took to the sky for the first time. Charles soon got a job "barn-storming"—giving flying demonstrations to people who had never seen an airplane before. He called himself "Daredevil Lindbergh" and would gather crowds by walking out on the wing while another pilot flew the plane over farm fields and small towns.

Spirit of St. Louis

The *Spirit of St. Louis* was the single-engine aircraft that Charles Lindbergh piloted alone on May 20-21, 1927. It had been built like no other plane before or since.

Charles had the fuel tank put in front of the pilot's seat instead of behind it, so he would not be stuck between the tank and the engine if he had to crash-land. However, having the fuel tank in front meant that there could be no front window. Charles could see what was ahead only by peering through a periscope or leaning out of the side window. To keep the plane light, so it could fly farther on less fuel, he flew without a radio, lights, or parachute.

The *Spirit of St. Louis* is now on display at the Smithsonian National Air and Space Museum in Washington, D.C.

To learn all he could about aviation, Charles joined the Army Air Service Reserve. In 1926, he graduated first in his class, then took a job as an airmail pilot. At the time, that was the most dangerous job in the country: 31 of the first 40 airmail pilots died in crashes. Charles survived two crashes, then decided to move on.

Like every other pilot in the country, Charles had been paying close attention to the competition for the Orteig Prize. In 1919, Raymond Orteig, a hotel magnate, had offered to pay $25,000 to any aviator who could fly nonstop between New York and Paris, in either direction. By 1926, no one had come close.

Charles emptied his bank account and went to seek investors in St. Louis, where he had become famous as an airmail pilot. He bought a plane and named it the *Spirit of St. Louis*, in honor of his investors. He designed special changes to make it as light-weight and fuel-efficient as possible.

All the other pilots aiming for the Orteig Prize had flown with at least one co-pilot, but Charles planned to try it alone. On May 10, 1927, he boarded his plane in San Diego and headed for New York. When he landed at

Roosevelt Field on Long Island, New York, newspaper reporters were charging down the runway even before the propellers stopped turning. The idea that someone would dare to try flying across the Atlantic was big news—especially since two teams attempting the same feat had crashed recently. Charles seemed so unlikely to make it to Paris that newspapers were calling him "The Flying Fool."

Rain kept Charles on the ground until May 20, when he climbed aboard the *Spirit of St. Louis* and took off. Few people believed that he would ever be seen again. Today, flying across the Atlantic is safe, comfortable, and commonplace. In Charles's time, however, it was so dangerous that few people dared to try it. Charles was all alone in a small craft. He had no radio for communication, no heat, no lights, no parachute, and only basic navigation equipment. He had to stay awake the entire time, too, or he would crash into the ocean.

Somehow, his courage and sheer will to succeed carried him through. After 3,600 miles and 33-1/2 hours in the air, he succeeded where no one ever had before. From the moment he

"Success is not measured by what a man accomplishes, but by the opposition he has encountered, and the courage with which he maintained the struggle against overwhelming odds."
—Charles Lindbergh

The Lone Eagle: Charles Lindbergh in 1927

landed his plane just outside of Paris, "the Lone Eagle" was the most famous man in the world. U.S. President Calvin Coolidge sent a battleship to bring him home and four million people turned out to meet it when it reached New York. Mobs chased Charles everywhere he went, desperate for a glimpse of the courageous young man—dubbed "Lucky Lindy"—who had conquered the skies.

A Hero's Heartache

Being a beloved hero did not spare Charles from tragedy. In 1932, his infant son was kidnapped and found dead 72 hours later. Charles's celebrity status turned that personal tragedy into headline news. To escape the media circus of the investigation and trial, Charles eventually moved his family to England.

Lindbergh's historic solo flight was celebrated in many ways around the country, including this ticker-tape parade in New York City on June 13, 1927.

Charles lost many admirers when he joined a group that opposed U.S. participation in World War II. When the U.S. did enter the war in 1941, however, he offered his services to the Air Force and flew combat missions against the Japanese.

In time, Charles regained his popularity. *The Spirit of St. Louis*, the book he wrote about his famous flight, won a Pulitzer Prize.

Charles Lindbergh died at age 72, at his home in Hawaii. Remembered for his historic transatlantic flight, he remains a symbol of courage and daring.

Life Lines

1902 Charles Augustus Lindbergh is born in Detroit, Michigan, on February 4. The following year, Orville and Wilbur Wright make the first-ever sustained piloted airplane flight.

1927 On May 20, Charles takes off from New York in the *Spirit of St. Louis*. On May 21, he lands near Paris, becoming the first person to make a nonstop solo flight across the Atlantic Ocean.

1935 Charles moves his family to England to escape media scrutiny.

1944-1945 Charles flies combat missions in support of U.S. troops fighting in the Pacific during World War II.

1954 Charles's autobiography, *The Spirit of St. Louis,* wins a Pulitzer Prize.

1974 Charles Lindbergh dies of cancer in Hawaii on August 26.

November 1960: Ruby Bridges, with U.S. deputy marshals protecting her from protesters, leaves William Frantz Elementary after a day at school.

Ruby Bridges

born 1954

The year was 1960. Clutching her mother's hand on one side and a federal marshal's hand on the other, six-year-old Ruby Bridges marched bravely up the steps of the William Frantz School in New Orleans, Louisiana. The school was surrounded by a crowd of angry protesters chanting racist slurs at her. Until that day, New Orleans had had segregated (separate) schools for blacks and whites. When Ruby walked through that school door, she became one of the first black children in the South to attend the same public school as white children. Her courage helped change America.

A Historic Decision

On May 17, 1954, the U.S. Supreme Court handed down its decision in a case called *Brown* v. *the Board of Education of Topeka, Kansas*. By a 9-to-0 vote, the Court ordered an end to segregation in public schools. A few months after that historic ruling, Ruby Nell Bridges was born in Tylertown, Mississippi.

Ruby's parents were living on a cotton farm, where they worked hard but earned very little money. The day before Ruby's birth, her mother was in the fields, carting a 90-pound load of cotton on her back. In search of a better life, the Bridges family moved to the city of New Orleans, Louisiana.

When Ruby was old enough for school, her parents enrolled her in an all-black public kindergarten. That year, 1959, a federal court judge ordered New Orleans to follow the Supreme Court's 1954 ruling by immediately ending its practice of segregating schools by race. The following spring, all of the city's African American kindergartners took a test to see who would go to an integrated (mixed-race) school in the fall.

Ruby passed the test, and she was one of six African American children chosen to integrate the schools. Ruby and two other black students were slated to attend the all-white William Frantz School. The other three were to attend a different white school. At the last minute, however, the two children who were to join Ruby at William Frantz backed out. She would be integrating the school on her own.

In a Class By Herself

On the morning of November 14, 1960, federal marshals showed up at Ruby's door. They had come to keep Ruby and her mother safe on their way to the school. Ruby had no idea what she was about to face: Her mother had told her only that she was going to a different school, and that there might be a crowd of people there.

Ruby, her mother, and the marshals pushed through a crowd of angry, insulting protesters and made their way to the principal's office. Ruby sat there all day, watching as white parents arrived to take their children out of the building because they did not want them attending school with a black child.

The next day, the marshals took Ruby and her mother to school again. The crowd was even bigger and angrier. This time, however, a young white woman met Ruby and her mother at the

"She showed a lot of courage. She never cried. She didn't whimper. She just marched along like a little soldier. And we're all very proud of her."
—Charles Burks, one of the U.S. marshals who escorted Ruby Bridges through the mob on her first day at William Frantz School

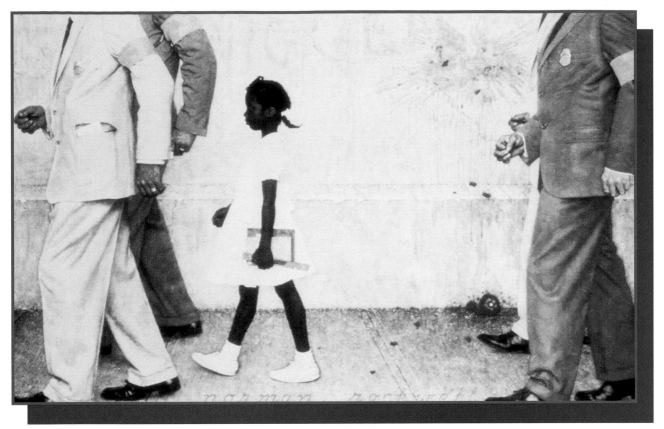

In 1964, Norman Rockwell—a famous illustrator—painted this picture of Ruby Bridges being escorted to school. Its title, The Problem We All Live With, *refers to racism in the U.S.*

door. She was Barbara Henry, Ruby's teacher. She kindly led Ruby to a classroom. It was empty, but Mrs. Henry held class, anyway—for Ruby alone. For most of that school year, Ruby was the only student in Mrs. Henry's class. Most of the other children were kept home by their parents. The few first-graders who did attend had been placed by the principal in a different class.

Not many first-graders would have had the courage to face down angry protesters without tears or to attend school with no friends. Ruby Bridges did have it. She did not back down, not once. She did not miss a single day of school that year.

Ruby's strength paid off. When she returned to William Frantz for second grade, there were no protesters, and she attended class with 20 other children—some black, some white. Thanks to Ruby and the three children who had integrated the other school, segregated education in New Orleans was coming to an end.

Ruby Bridges went on to become a travel agent. She married and had four sons. She rarely talked about her role in helping to end segregation. When her brother was killed in the early 1990s,

Ruby Bridges-Hall with Barbara Henry, her first-grade teacher—38 years later

Ruby's Teacher

Ruby Bridges-Hall says that she would not have made it through first grade without the love and support of her teacher, Barbara Henry.

Barbara had moved to New Orleans from Boston two months before Ruby enrolled at the school. Barbara did all she could to make Ruby's school life normal. Ruby was not allowed to go out for recess or to the cafeteria, so Barbara played jacks with her in the classroom and often sat with her at lunchtime.

In 1996, Ruby and Barbara met for the first time in 35 years, while taping the *Oprah Winfrey* show. Today, Barbara visits schools, talking about Ruby to let kids know that "they, too, can do very important things and they, too, can be heroes."

however, Ruby looked back on her own life. She realized that what she had done was important. She now runs the Ruby Bridges Foundation, an organization that helps poor children receive a better education. She also travels throughout the country, giving speeches about her experiences. Ruby hopes that people who hear her story will be inspired to find the courage to work against injustice wherever they see it.

"Our Ruby taught us all a lot," said Lucille Bridges, Ruby's mother. "She became someone who helped change our country. She was part of history, just like generals and presidents are part of history. They're leaders, and so was Ruby. She led us away from hate, and she led us nearer to knowing each other, the white folks and the black folks."

Life Lines

1954 On May 17, the U.S. Supreme Court outlaws segregation in public schools in its *Brown* v. *Board of Education* ruling. On September 8, Ruby Nell Bridges is born in Tylertown, Mississippi.

1960 In July, a federal court in New Orleans orders two white public schools to follow the law and admit black children. Ruby Bridges is chosen to be one of the black students to attend William Frantz School, an all-white elementary school in New Orleans. On November 14, she enrolls at William Frantz School, becoming one of the first African American children to desegregate a public school in the South.

1998 *Ruby Bridges*, a made-for-TV movie about Ruby's experiences, airs.

1999 Ruby publishes *Through My Eyes*, an autobiography written for children.